Dinosaur

Gregory McNamee, SERIES EDITOR

Dinosaur

Four Seasons on the Green and Yampa Rivers

TEXT BY Hal Crimmel

PHOTOGRAPHS BY Steve Gaffney

The University of Arizona Press   Tucson

The University of Arizona Press
Text © 2007 Hal Crimmel
Photographs © 2007 Steve Gaffney
This book is printed on acid-free, archival-quality paper.
Manufactured in the United States of America

12 11 10 09 08 07   6 5 4 3 2 1

Library of Congress Cataloging-in-Publication Data appear
on the last printed page of this book.

Frontispiece: Little Rainbow Park and the head of Split
Mountain Canyon, Green River

contents

CONTENTS

viii

illustrations

ILLUSTRATIONS

X

acknowledgments

Current and former Dinosaur National Monument personnel lent generous assistance during the last several years. I want to thank Janet Atwood, Steve Cunningham, Mike Haubert, James Heller, Kara King, Tamara Naumann, Dave Panabaker, Steve Petersburg, Wayne Prokopetz, Mark Rosenthal, Doug Ross, Matt Sandate, Sue Walter, Michael Weinstein, and David Whitman.

Others who assisted with this book include Sean Abbott, Mark Biddle, Russ Burrows, Henry Crimmel, Ann Elmer, Sue Hinebauch, Herm Hoops, Mark H. Fuller at the U.S. Fish and Wildlife Service in Vernal, Kim Grob, Charlie Mantle, Ed and Melanie Morrison at River Runners'

Transport in Vernal, and Catharine and Marty Shields. Desert Places series editor Greg McNamec helped with the proposal. Lastly, I am grateful to Patti Hartmann, senior editor at the University of Arizona Press, for her professionalism and encouragement.

Support for this project was provided by the John A. and Telitha E. Lindquist Endowment for Creative and Artistic Endeavors at Weber State University, by the Charles Redd Center for Western Studies at Brigham Young University, and by the Research, Scholarship, and Professional Growth Committee at Weber State University.

Dinosaur

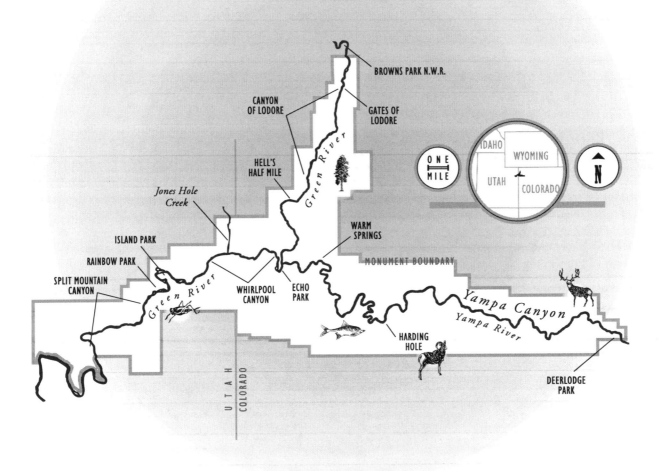

BROWNS PARK N.W.R.

CANYON
OF LODORE

GATES OF
LODORE

HELL'S
HALF MILE

Green River

*Jones Hole
Creek*

ISLAND PARK

WARM
SPRINGS

RAINBOW PARK

MONUMENT BOUNDARY

SPLIT MOUNTAIN
CANYON

Green River

WHIRLPOOL
CANYON

ECHO
PARK

Yampa Canyon

Yampa River

HARDING
HOLE

DEERLODGE
PARK

UTAH
COLORADO

ONE
MILE

IDAHO   WYOMING

UTAH   COLORADO

N

Map of Dinosaur National Monument

Dinosaur: a high desert oasis

The absence of water may define many desert places, but the presence of water defines the high desert oasis of Dinosaur National Monument. In the following pages, photographer Steve Gaffney and I share our impressions of Dinosaur's Green and Yampa rivers and the lands they flow through. The ever-changing magic of water and sky, we discovered, exists here in all four seasons.

On our whitewater river trips and hikes we realized that the personal vision of place expressed in this book would be incomplete without discussing the pressures facing the monument. Like most wild areas, desert places are at risk, and desert rivers especially so. We hope this book communicates not only the beauty of Dinosaur's rivers, canyons, and parks, but also the threats to them.

a season of ice: the monument in winter

The bitterest winter days scrape forty below in Dinosaur National Monument's high cold desert, a spare country of sagebrush and stone, pinyon and juniper, rivers and canyons, of solitude in the right place and season. On this January night at the mouth of Split Mountain Canyon, the temperature is a relatively mild two degrees, with just a sliver of low-lying moon in the immense star-filled western sky. Huge platelets of frazil ice, slushy floes formed in turbulent water on clear cold nights, scuff the shore where the Green River gurgles beneath big cottonwoods.

Downstream, bank-to-bank ice swallows dark water. Snow might fall, but I am not optimistic. The monument lies in the precipitation shadow of high ranges: to the northwest, the nearby Uintas, running east-west for 160 miles along the Utah-Wyoming border, and to the west, the north-south trending Wasatch Mountains, east of Salt Lake City, 150 miles away. With multiple peaks above ten thousand feet, the mountains wring so much moisture from winter storms blowing east that parts of Dinosaur receive as little as fifteen inches of snow annually, versus three hundred inches in the Uinta high country and five hundred-plus in the upper Wasatch.

Steve and I savor this chance to enjoy Dinosaur's winter moods and explore places most visitors see only in summer, when these semiarid lands shimmer with intense, bewildering heat, often soaring above one hundred degrees. Tonight the only heat comes from the glowing campfire; beyond it windswept steppe, isolated canyons, dry washes, and rock stretch into the night in all directions. Neither Steve nor I call these tough borderlands of northeastern Utah and northwestern Colorado home. But cold, remoteness, and border country feel right. We both grew up about a hundred miles from the nearest city, in a rural New York county near the Canadian line, a place of rivers and snow. Steve is an old friend and photographer with an eclectic background. He's operated safaris on Kenya's Masai Mara, been a personal trainer for Hollywood celebrities, and similar to a jazz musician, he improvises at a moment's notice—an ideal partner in exploration. Over the last decade we lost track of each other, but standing around outside on a winter's night is a familiar activity that makes it seem as if only weeks have passed. We drink cold Molson, relishing the coppery bite of ale. "Drinking half-frozen beer out on the railroad tracks on a Saturday night, that's what this reminds me of," says Steve, recalling our small-town roots.

Like many raised in rural places, I now find city life appealing, yet a love of remote rivers persists. And the monument is an ideal place to find them. Lying in a high desert eddy, in a forgotten corner of the intermountain

Winter morning on the Green River, mouth of Split Mountain Canyon

West, the monument is a half-day's drive from the nearest major city, over high ranges and across sparsely populated sagebrush country—an American outback. Dinosaur sits on the edge of three major regions: Rocky Mountain, Basin and Range, and Colorado Plateau, the latter a geologically diverse, semiarid tableland radiating from the Four Corners region. Hydrologically speaking, Dinosaur lies in the 245,000-square-mile Colorado Basin, that snowmelt-fed web of rivers heading in the high mountains of Wyoming, Colorado, and Utah. Anchored by the Colorado River and draining toward the Gulf of California, the Colorado Basin contains such rivers as the San Juan, Dolores, White, Green, and Yampa.

Desert. Plateau. Basin. The words evoke mystery, distance, discovery. All exist on the monument's two extraordinary rivers: the storied Green, its basin sprawling across 45,000 square miles in Wyoming and Utah, and the majestic Yampa, draining 9,500 square miles in Colorado, Utah, and Wyoming. The Yampa survives as the only large free-flowing river in the desert West, no small feat in a region where most water was married off to a turbine decades ago. In Dinosaur, the Green River enters at the monument's northern tip, and the Yampa enters from the eastern side. The two rivers join at Echo Park near the monument's center, then flow west, exiting park service lands just south of Split Mountain, where Steve and I are camped. The two rivers have carved four extraordinary canyons: Lodore, Whirlpool, Split Mountain, and Yampa. For me, a river runner, the magic of Dinosaur National Monument lies in these canyons and the open spaces between them, known as parks.

Tonight, the cold air is heavy with scents of river and sage. I rub a pinch of the wintery leaves together and breathe in. As do fresh oysters on the half shell, crushed sage hints of brine, a reminder of salt spray that once drifted across prehistoric beaches during the region's marine past when oceans advanced and retreated twelve times. Shallow waters deposited the monument's limestone layers that alternate with sandstone and shale. Great plates shifted the land steadily, imperceptibly, like a geological trickster. Landscapes ranged from Saharan-style desert to subtropical swamps, plains, and lakes. "Here" is a relative concept, since the fossilized dunes of Weber Sandstone that form the mouth of Split Mountain once lay hundreds of miles south. Dinosaur is not fixed in time or space. Like the rivers, it is fluid, shifting matter and energy through the slow drift of geologic time.

Seas receded 150 million years ago, and the land gradually transitioned to become a place of rivers and dinosaurs. In a subtropical landscape dominated by palms and tree ferns, dozens of dinosaur species, including *Allosaurus*, a fierce meat eater, *Stegosaurus*, with its spiky spinal plates, and the thirty-ton plant-eating *Apatosaurus*, shared habitat with freshwater crocodiles, turtles, and other reptiles. The ancient rivers were life-giving, but also life-taking, as the flood-twisted fossils here attest. Paleontologists believe drowned animal carcasses jammed together like driftwood and were covered with sand and silt. The sediments compressed and hardened, and bones fossilized in what is now termed the Morrison Formation. Some layers eventually dove a mile into the earth's crust. Uplift exposed remains of animals with fire-hydrant-sized vertebrae, such as *Apatosaurus*, whose individual daily plant consumption matched that of a small cattle herd. Even so, the giant herbivores left enough plant life behind to keep the natural gas and crude oil flowing out of wells around the energy boomtown of Vernal. For instance, every gallon of gasoline refined from that crude oil began as 196,000 pounds—ninety-eight tons—of plant matter, more than enough to keep the most gluttonous beast in greens for a week. Nature's potential to compress so much into so little makes the presence of the intact dinosaur fossils found in the monument seem an extraordinary quirk of nature.

Just a few miles from where Steve and I are camped at Split Mountain lies the world's most significant Jurassic-era dinosaur quarry, the monument's namesake. The quarry was discovered on a hot August day nearly one hundred years ago, when Earl Douglass was poking around, hunting fossil specimens for the new wing of the Carnegie Museum in Pittsburgh. Along a ridge where the current visitor center and quarry exhibit lie, Douglass found the tip of a fossil iceberg: eight *Apatosaurus* tail vertebrae in perfect position. Later, over 350 tons of dinosaur fossils were unearthed; most would be removed and shipped east over the next several years. To preserve the remaining deposits of the now-famous quarry, with its exposed fossil-studded rock face, a presidential proclamation established the monument on eighty acres in 1915.

Years passed before the monument expanded to its current erratic shape, approximating a jagged inverted T. The shape is a result of monument expansions designed to protect the singular canyons on the Green and Yampa rivers and the surrounding plateau country. In 1938 the federal government expanded Dinosaur to 203,885 acres in Utah and Colorado; in 1960 the monument was enlarged to its present 211,141 acres.

Many wilderness groups would like to have another 120,000 acres added to the monument in order to protect surrounding lands. This nearby desert shrub country can lack the picturesque features that typically help garner support for federal protection, but places such as Bull Canyon, Cold Springs Mountain, archaeologically significant Daniels Canyon, and Diamond Breaks are necessary for maintaining Dinosaur's wild essence. Among other advantages, adding these places to the monument would further protect the watershed and preserve vistas from oil and gas development. Wildlife would benefit too. Predators such as mountain lions and bobcats and ungulates such as Rocky Mountain bighorn, elk, and mule deer would have greater room to roam.

Yet regional opposition to monument expansion is strong. In a movement similar to the anti-federal, anti-environmental sentiments of the 1970s Sagebrush Rebellion, counties adjacent to the monument and throughout the West are turning to a Civil War–era right-of-way law, in order to foil expansion of wilderness areas and fragment lands managed by the park service. Revised Statute 2477, or RS 2477, as it is known, authorizes counties to claim ownership and maintain rights-of-way that show historical use as highways, even if found on federal lands earmarked for listing as federally protected wilderness. Nearby Moffat County, Colorado, for instance, has filed claims for over two thousand miles of highways that cross federal land, including 240 miles in the monument. Many of these highways are little more than cow trails and streambeds. In one case, the "highway" is Yampa Canyon itself.

After a clear and cold night—with the temperature hovering around zero Fahrenheit—Steve and I wake to find the breakfast bananas rock hard. The once parrot-yellow fruit is now a gangrenous purplish black, and everything is frozen solid except that greasy staple of winter camping, bacon. Soon, the skillet snaps with hot fat, and we plan the day. Because the frozen rivers are impassible by boat, and many other parts of the monument are inaccessible in winter, Steve and I intend to explore several of the parks, those flat open areas nestled between the mouth of one canyon and the head of another. The best known are Browns Park, at the monument's northern tip, Deerlodge Park at the eastern end, Echo Park at the confluence of the Green and Yampa, and Island, Rainbow, and Little Rainbow parks downstream. Dinosaur's rivers typically meander through the parks, providing ideal wildlife habitat.

We pack a lunch, then drive around the monument's western tip, before turning east toward Rainbow Park, named after the weathered red, purple, green, and yellow shales of the Morrison Formation. Rainbow Park is textbook high desert. It is pinyon-juniper and sagebrush country, a spread of dry hills and sky stretching away to nothing, where clumps of vegetation are but black dots on a gray canvas. The sense of solitude is invigorating, even if the stark landscape suggests an animal turned out of its skin.

Steve and I leave the car and walk down to the Green River, which was originally known to the Shoshone and Crow as Seeds-ke-dee-agie, a word translated as Sage Hen or Prairie Hen River. The river later was named Río de San Buenaventura—the River of Good Fortune—by Fathers Dominguez and Escalante, who led an expedition seeking a route from Santa Fe to Alta California in 1776. The expedition successfully forded the Green downstream of Split Mountain Canyon, but the expedition's mapmaker, don Bernardo de Miera y Pacheco, wishfully drew the Green flowing to the Pacific, instead of to the south, where it joins the Colorado River north of Moab, Utah. In 1811 the famous German explorer and botanical geographer Alexander von Humboldt copied Pacheco's maps in Mexico City, thinking them accurate, and nearly a half-century more passed before the myth of an easy route to the Pacific died. Though fur trappers preferred the name Río Verde, or Green River, the notion of the river as a source of good fortune persists for river and desert aficionados.

This morning pancakes of frazil ice drift out of Rainbow Park, accenting the turbid green water slipping past the snow-covered shoreline. Winter brings out the best in color, and when the January sun crests the ridge to the south, the morning comes alive in a display of brilliant blue sky, green junipers, and red soil. Arcs of uplifted rock just downstream mark where the Green River leaves Little Rainbow Park and enters eight-mile-long Split Mountain Canyon, popular with river runners. But since it is winter, Steve and I decide to head for Whirlpool Canyon to try and explore upstream on the ice. We leave Rainbow Park traveling north and west toward Island Park, named for its many islands. The sun climbs in the sky, turning the snow-dusted road to greasy, sticky mud, and we'll have to be careful not to get stuck. I wish this area was roadless. But at least the roads are still dirt. How much better their roughness fits the land than asphalt.

Soon we are walking toward the mouth of Whirlpool Canyon, where the Green enters Island Park. Along the way we cross the abandoned Ruple Ranch, with its sun-dried corral and sagging buildings. Settled in 1883 and worked into the 1950s, the ranch is a monument to isolation and staying power. Arriving at the riverbank, Steve and I find it lined with what appear to be thousands of glittering translucent crocuses. These delicate white crystalline shapes are rime ice, created when objects are exposed to freezing fog, common along Dinosaur's rivers in the winter months. Around the corner upstream, in the deep shade of the canyon, the rime ice yields to solid opaque ice—an ideal surface to walk.

Steve decides to photograph at the canyon mouth, so I head upstream on the ice encasing the river bank to bank. I'd once read that in the winter of 1838, trapper Joe Meek rode a horse one hundred miles on the frozen Green River from Browns Park on the monument's northern extremity to the Green's confluence with the White River far downstream from Split Mountain. I believe the story now. I'm intrigued by the idea of riding a horse down a frozen desert river, especially since I'm accustomed as a rafter to associate western canyons with boats and heat.

Corral at Ruple Ranch and mouth of Whirlpool Canyon

Green River from the Island Park Overlook

I am also intrigued by the surprising amount of ecological diversity found in the short distance I've walked in the last hour. I started in Island Park's sagebrush and cottonwoods but am now looking at Whirlpool Canyon's stately Douglas fir, a mountain species. In fact, Dinosaur is known for its diverse ecosystems. "Life communities," formerly called "life zones," are groups of ecological niches defined by elevation and exposure to sunshine. The sun is such a factor in canyon ecosystems that the same life community on the southern slope of a canyon might exist only one thousand feet lower on the northern slope of that same canyon. In Dinosaur, seven communities exist: the aquatic and riparian, both below 5,500 feet elevation; the protected cliff and ledge; and the desert shrub community, with its limited precipitation, searing summers, and cold winters. Above these are the pinyon-juniper and mountain-shrub communities, stretching to the snowy montane community above 8,000 feet, formerly known as the Canadian life zone. This January, winter has settled in along the river, and finding ice and subarctic cold in the high desert is satisfying. With a renewed appreciation for this place, I walk back to join Steve.

The January sun tumbles out of the sky, and soon monochrome dusk settles across Island Park as bands of approaching clouds fill the horizon. In subsequent winter trips Steve and I find fifty-head herds of elk wintering along the river across from Tree Island, where tangerine light from the setting sun reflects off exposed cliffs. Tonight, though, we drive on the refrozen road through the sweep of sagebrush back to Split Mountain campground.

Under a cloudy sky filling with smoke-dry snow, the Green River is still at it, eroding the gaping sandstone mouth of Split Mountain, portentous, puzzling in the night. Did the river saw through the rock as the layers were slowly uplifted, a process called antecedence? Or did it cut through a thick ancient bed of gravel to the Split Mountain Anticline, a buried rock dome, then carve out the eight-mile Split Mountain Canyon? Geologists favor the latter interpretation, but whatever the case this river existed in some form 25 million years ago during the late Oligocene–early Miocene era.

I relish camping next to such an ancient river, with its murmuring water. And I like the cold and ice on this January night. The weather gives Dinosaur's rugged high desert an even harder edge. This expansive sun-seared country where the Great Basin Desert reaches for the Rockies, where conifers stipple rock like ticks on a burro, where the sharp bloom of cactus flowers splashes the earth with spring color is not yet my own. But tonight, near the monument's lowest point at 4,730 feet, the familiar patterns of river and cold offer a homecoming of sorts, one that brings me back to the long cold winters of my youth.

high water and wingless protein:
a spring journey

In May and June, Split Mountain campground has an entirely different ambience. Instead of silence and ice, the snowmelt-fed Green River becomes filled bank to bank with turbulent brown water. Riverside bushes are a-whirrp with randy birds, making the campground a birder's paradise. River runners rendezvous for trips on the Green and Yampa; those concluding trips take out here as well.

The growth of rafting in the monument can be traced back to World War II, when military surplus rubber rafts made taking customers safely down Dinosaur's rivers economically feasible. Vernal residents Bus Hatch and Frank Swain realized the boats' potential, and by 1956 the two men were launching ten-day trips in Green River, Wyoming, and taking out downstream from Split Mountain, near Jensen, Utah. In the 1960s rafting became more popular in the monument, and the canyons grew crowded. In 1972 the park service capped river use at fourteen thousand people annually and implemented a lottery-based permit system to maintain a quality wilderness experience. Today, heavy demand means lottery participants for private noncommercial trips have as little as a 3 percent chance of securing high-water launches in May and June, especially on the Yampa. The upside is that the limited number of launches prevents overcrowding, and the lucky few who draw a permit gain a measure of solitude and wildness, and a dose of whitewater.

Running the Yampa at high water had been a decade-long dream of mine. As an easterner, something about the exotic-sounding name, Yampa, always appealed to me, though the yampa plant, the river's namesake, is related to the humble carrot. Yampa (*Perideridia gairdneri*) can reach a height of two feet, is high in iron and carotene, and has loads of protein and carbohydrates. The nutritious plant was a staple food of the Yamparicas, a Ute band who inhabited the region.

Yampa roots provided physical nourishment then; today the Yampa River, as the only remaining major free-flowing river in the Colorado River system, provides spiritual nourishment to lovers of wildness and free-flowing water. South of Steamboat Springs, Colorado, the Yampa begins gathering on the White River Plateau, winds across the Yampa Valley and through a series of canyons, then drops through the famed Cross Mountain Gorge, an expert kayak run. After entering Lily Park, the Yampa meanders to the monument boundary at Deerlodge Park, the put-in for river trips.

When the opportunity finally arose to take a private six-day June Yampa trip with a group of friends, I couldn't wait to float the river forty-six miles west to its confluence with the Green at Echo Park, then continue another twenty-six miles to the takeout at Split Mountain. I found the essence of springtime rivers on this trip in the form of Warm Springs Rapid and a plague of crickets.

After loading the rafts under a hot sun, our mixed group of nine women and men left Deerlodge Park behind and floated into the upper canyon. Dominated by the 300-million-year-old Pennsylvanian Morgan Formation, formed of shallow reef-strewn seas, the first twenty-four miles of the Yampa is a whitewater bonanza. Owing to a gradient of seventeen feet per mile—relatively high for a large desert river—this upper section is filled with rapids such as Tepee, Little Joe, and Big Joe. When the water runs above five or six thousand cubic feet per second (cfs)—the standard measure of river flow—the Yampa fills with tossing waves and steady whitewater.

Our trip put in on 8,500 cfs, meaning that Warm Springs Rapid, twenty miles downstream of Big Joe, would cast a cautionary note over the trip. More than four decades ago, on June 10, 1965, a debris flow of mud and rock thundered down Warm Springs Draw. Weeks of exceptionally heavy rain caused the soil to liquefy and avalanche into the river, where the water backed up behind the natural dam. The river finally broke through the next morning, forming a major new rapid. A two-boat Hatch River Expeditions trip was the first to discover it. At the oars on the lead raft, guide Les Oldham was not expecting to find anything unusual on this stretch of river, and he was not wearing his lifejacket. Suddenly a ferocious new rapid grabbed Oldham's raft, and when the boat cleared the rapid, the passengers noticed their oarsman was missing. Oldham, who had been washed overboard at some point, never resurfaced. His would be the first of several lives Warm Springs would claim in the next forty years.

Decades of spring floods cleared much of the debris, making Warm Springs a little less deadly. It is still considered one of the West's famous "big drops," and remains a feared class IV, with most of the river feeding Maytag, an explosive hole. Rapids are rated on a scale of easy, class I, to nearly impossible, class VI. The Yampa's spring whitewater tends toward the middle ranges—runnable, but with consequences.

After several days on the river, our nine-person group pulled ashore to scout Warm Springs carefully, not wanting to end upside down in Maytag. The worst-case scenario was obvious: Missing the correct line meant the raft would slam into Maytag's whitewater wall and flip, tossing everyone into the rapid. Initially, the hole might pull people underwater, but their lifejackets would pop them to the surface downstream. The swim would be bad but not fatal, we all agreed, before climbing back into the two fifteen-foot rafts.

At the oars in the lead raft, I drifted into position, then began rowing hard. The raft accelerated in the current rushing toward Maytag, as the roar from the hole grew in intensity. Cold spray from the aerated water enveloped the raft, and I pulled at the oars as Maytag's white froth grew closer. The raft bucked and shuddered as we broke through the diagonal waves feeding the hole on the river right side (using a downstream orientation, boaters use the terms "river right" or "river left" to identify routes through rapids), and then, suddenly, we were past the thunderous thing.

The second raft ran an identically clean line, but then a gust of up-stream wind skidded the boats across the river. I looked upstream. In white-water, it is not always what happened that makes a story; it's what could have happened. Had we run Warm Springs a minute later, the wind might have blown a raft directly into Maytag, with disastrous results.

The combination of luck and choice make rapids a place of infinite out-comes. Later that afternoon our group camped two miles downstream from Warm Springs at Box Elder Park, where we had a chance to witness the fallout of a missed line at Warm Springs. Oars, multicolored flotsam, and a cooler bobbed by, headed for Lake Powell. Eventually a raft raced around the bend, chasing the runaway yard sale. "We wanted to clip the edge of the hole but dropped right into the middle of it," shouted a sodden rafter, as one of our group, bathing au naturel, scurried onto a sandbar to return an oar salvaged from the current.

Perhaps it's the combination of the desert's elemental beauty and the soft-core petroglyphs found throughout canyons in the Colorado Basin that unlocks one's inner nudist. Or maybe it's the surge of whitewater-induced adrenaline that causes rivers to cut to psychic bedrock, inciting many to cast off convention.

The next few days took us to the confluence with the Green at Echo Park, through Whirlpool Canyon, and on through the flatwater of Island and Rainbow parks. As the head of Split Mountain Canyon drew near, the heat became secondary to a pulsating wall-to-wall carpet of Mormon crickets (*Anabrus simplex*), wingless grasshoppers on steroids. Thousands and thousands of these glittering crunchy little breakfast sausages with legs overran beaches and blanketed the water. The creepy mass migration was an insectophile's fantasy and a fundamentalist's confirmation of evil rolled into one.

Trying to ignore the insects, we floated downstream, anticipating predictable rapids: Moonshine, S.O.B., Schoolboy. Moonshine, however, caught us by surprise. It narrowed into powerful compression waves, flipped a raft end over end, and dumped the crew into heavy water. The swimmers battled current and crickets, as the river exacted revenge for the clean lines at Warm Springs. By the time we had rescued everyone, the discerning critters had crawled into swimmers' bikini tops, lifejackets, and long hair. Picked off and flung into the swollen river, the doomed insects protested with sickly croaking chirps.

Though Mormon cricket outbreaks are part of the region's natural history, their barbaric habits—swarming towns, ravaging gardens, cannibalizing one another on carcass-slickened roads—never won fans in the Great Basin. Crickets go through seven developmental stages, called instars. After the fourth instar they gang up like teenagers and begin migrating up to a mile per day. The dense bands eat everything in their path. They prefer fungi and nongrass plants but will devour rangeland grasses and crops such as alfalfa, wheat, and barley, destroying the livelihoods of farmers and ranchers. Following a severe drought and overgrazing in the 1930s, for example, crickets played a significant factor in the demise of small dry-land ranches.

More recently, in the 1980s, the U.S. Department of Agriculture tried to control outbreaks by spraying the oily insecticide Sevin. Over thirteen million acres were treated one year, among them thousands near the monument. Wildlife suffered, especially peregrine falcons, whose food supply was destroyed. Sevin left dead zones, devoid of crickets and other insects usually eaten by the songbirds that peregrine falcons hunted. Falcon populations plummeted. This Sevin-induced disaster suggests that the more humans seek to perfect nature by eliminating its undesirable aspects, the more elusive perfection becomes. Think of hydroponic tomatoes, toupees, Michael Jackson.

Fremont, Ute, and Shoshone peoples had a different approach to insect control. They caught, roasted, and ate the protein-rich crickets. Revolting? Surely no worse than a Big Mac. For us that day, an all-you-can-eat buffet of drowned and living insects swirled in the current. The most determined to live sought refuge on the rafts. Preferring cold cuts to hard-shelled insects, the crew beat them back with river sandals and a kayak paddle.

The exact cause of cricket outbreaks remains a mystery. But mass migrations of so-called undesirable species in this age of order and control are remarkable. The fact that lands in and around the monument give birth to crickets speaks to the country's remoteness. The wildness these insects represent is darkly fascinating. Oddly enough, they complement the swollen Green River, fed by snowmelt from the unfettered Yampa.

a quest for solitude: summer in the Canyon of Lodore

In the month of August the Green River drifts slowly through Browns Park, a sprawling valley at the monument's northern tip. Prior to settlement, tribes wintering in Browns Park—Comanche, Shoshone, and Ute—called the place O-wi-yu-kuts, meaning "Big Valley." Fur trappers arrived after 1800 and began to call the valley Browns Hole. Did the name originate with someone named Brown murdered by Indians, or another Brown forced to winter here after snows sealed off the mountain passes? The answer is unclear, but many feel the name originated with Baptiste Brown, a French-Canadian trapper who settled in the valley. In any event, homesteaders, ranchers, and cattle rustlers began arriving in the 1860s, and by 1869 the name Browns Park had stuck. In the era before federal law enforcement, Browns Park was a popular stop on the Outlaw Trail because three jurisdictions—Wyoming, Colorado, and Utah—intersected here. Renegades needed only to ride across the nearest border to escape pursuing lawmen. Butch Cassidy and the Sundance Kid, for instance, especially liked Browns Park for this reason.

Today, a portion of Browns Park adjacent to the monument contains the 13,455-acre Browns Park National Wildlife Refuge, with its populations of moose, elk, pronghorn, black bear, and mule deer. But the refuge is best known for its 220-plus species of migratory and breeding birds, including bald eagles, teal and canvasback ducks, white-faced ibis, and Clark's grebe.

The southeastern corner of Browns Park lies inside the monument, and this is where Green River trips launch. Releases from Flaming Gorge Dam forty-six miles upstream make the Green, which heads in Wyoming's storm-soaked Wind River Range, floatable all summer. On this busy August morning several groups of rafters, including Steve and me, prepare for the forty-four-mile run to the takeout near Split Mountain Campground.

Steve and I are here in the August heat to enjoy the Green at its laziest and to enjoy easy living in the canyons and parks downstream. We've been assigned the Wade and Curtis campsite, only a short three-mile float away, so we are in no hurry to finish loading our thirteen-foot self-bailing raft equipped with an oar frame. We will take turns rowing, giving me an opportunity to paddle some rapids in the whitewater kayak I'm strapping to the back of the raft.

After a ranger checks our gear to ensure it complies with regulations, we set off on the slow current toward the Gates of Lodore, a deep cut in the Uintas' eastern tip. With its high angular cliffs, the Gates of Lodore is a favorite nesting area for peregrine falcons, raptors that dive after prey at speeds exceeding two hundred miles per hour. Here and elsewhere in the monument, peregrines were successfully reintroduced in the 1980s, after DDT and the disastrous spraying of Sevin wiped out the population. Reintroduction required drastic measures, including a scenario where owls were dispatched by shotgun from a helicopter. Falcons compete with owls for habitat, and the park service felt reducing the owl population was the most effective way to help falcon populations recover. Today there are fifteen nesting peregrine pairs in the monument, with room for another five.

Soon Steve and I are nearing camp, and that is fine by me. I'm glad for the short float because it offers a chance to settle in and anticipate the miles to come. Once we are ashore in the midday heat, the lap of river gives way to silence, and sun bleaches the canyon until it resembles an overexposed photograph. Toward evening, as light ebbs, color will seep back into the landscape. But now, in the dry desert air—more absence than presence—I can almost feel water evaporating into the enameled blue sky of this abnormally dry cycle, the sixth year of the worst drought in five hundred years, that grips the Colorado River Basin. Tree-ring data suggest the region hasn't been this parched since the sixteenth century. Six hundred thousand acres of sagebrush, the hardy, opportunistic, exceptionally well-adapted plant as common to high desert as conifer is to boreal forest, have perished across the West.

As day glides toward evening, we set off on foot, exploring downcanyon. The descending tremolo of canyon wren, a most musical bird, calls us deeper into the canyon. The gorge tightens and the gradient increases, promising isolation and whitewater in coming days. Searing aromatic dry heat radiates from juniper and sage in late afternoon sun, and these high desert scents accompany us to Winnies Grotto. A scramble into this perpendicular cleft reveals an intimate red rock amphitheater soaring thousands of feet to the rim.

Returning to the river, we scout Winnies Rapid, the first in Lodore. Winnies looks innocuous, but the main channel flows into a notorious rock with a penchant for flipping rafts; we'll try our luck tomorrow. Steve and I backtrack to camp as the glowing red quartzite canyon walls darken slowly to merlot. This billion-year-old Precambrian rock is the oldest in the monument, and much of it is covered with smooth, shiny black patches of desert varnish, a thin coating of clays, oxides, iron, and manganese deposited on exposed rock surfaces in arid and semiarid environments. Recent studies of biofilms, thin organic layers found in desert varnish, suggest that bacteria and fungus also form or help form desert varnish. Especially striking in Dinosaur's canyons are the fanciful decorative patterns formed by these rock coatings.

After dinner Steve and I walk to the river's edge and plunge in. We wash off dust and sweat, feeling the cold shock of river at night. The swift current pulls at my legs, and the blood red canyon walls pull at my imagination, fusing dream and reality. Chilled from the swim, I get in my sleeping bag and lie there, feeling the weight of all that rock around me. Later that night I wake from dark dreams choked with crimes never committed, women I never knew. "The things of the night cannot be explained in the day because they do not then exist," wrote that master of shadows Ernest Hemingway, and I am grateful when morning finally breaks, clear and cool. Sun hits the western rim and creeps toward the river. The east wall glows deep red; a trick of reflected light brings out the rock's fiery heart. Like dreams, reflected light often reveals the most startling aspects of place.

A Botanical Rat

Next morning a woodpecker begins working a dead box elder. As its beak clacks against the tree in the morning quiet, a two-boat commercial trip rounds the corner, breaking the spell of solitude. The lead raft is oared by a lanky blond dude and bears down quickly. Paying guests bring up the rear in inflatable rubber kayaks.

It's hard to imagine that less than two hundred years ago fur trade fortune seeker General William Ashley came through here in bullboats, craft made of buffalo hides stretched over willow branches. Resembling large floating bird nests, bullboats waterlogged quickly and were not particularly maneuverable—definitely not ideal boats for running whitewater rivers. Still, the flexible boats, derived from craft used by Plains Indians, seemed serviceable enough that General Ashley decided to adapt them for his exploration of the Green River. Ashley disliked the original circular design, and he ordered long broad-beamed craft built. He floated downstream from southern Wyoming with seven men, emerging intact below Split Mountain days later. His was the first recorded account of running the Green River's canyons.

But the most historically significant exploration of the Green began on May 24, 1869. The now-famous one-armed Civil War veteran Major John Wesley Powell launched from Green River, Wyoming, with a crew of nine on the first of two expeditions. At the time the canyons of the Green and Colorado were little known, and Powell intended to fill in one of the few remaining blank spots on western maps. Fourteen days later, after successfully descending Flaming Gorge and Red Canyon, and then floating Browns Park, the expedition came to the gaping mouth of the canyon they named Lodore, after a poem by the Englishman Robert Southey. Lodore's steep drops would test their rowboats—three made of heavy oak and one of pine, each carrying about a ton of supplies.

Careening out of a difficult drop one June day in 1869, the water-filled *No Name* did not make it ashore before the next stretch of whitewater. Drawn into the head of the rapid, the wooden craft banged down the rocky channel, broached, filled with more water, broached again, and sank. The crew of three survived, but one ton of supplies and gear was lost, except for the expedition's barometers and the liquid mascot smuggled in by the crew: a three-gallon keg of whiskey. Powell, apparently not a fan of happy hour, would name the drop Disaster Falls.

Steve and I have no trouble running both Upper and Lower Disaster Falls in our high-tech modern-day raft at this low summer water level, and soon we drift up to a mattress-sized beach crowded with tamarisk, a fast-growing feathery shrublike tree imported from Asia. This plant, one of the monument's seventy-five nonnative floral species, has reached epidemic proportions on the Green River. Sometimes called saltcedar, tamarisk was introduced to America in the early nineteenth century as an ornamental plant. By midcentury it had gone feral, and by the 1920s ranchers were using it to control erosion along irrigation ditches. This was a disastrous case of the fox guarding the chicken coop. Tamarisk quickly spread into waterways, and today it infests roughly 1.5 million acres of riparian habitat in the western United States. Mature tamarisk gulp up to three hundred gallons of water daily, robbing native plants and trees such as cottonwoods of badly needed moisture. By some estimates, tamarisk consumes as much as 4.5 million acre-feet of water (an acre-foot, equal to 325,851 gallons, is the amount of water needed to cover one acre of land to a depth of one foot) each year in eleven western states, enough to supply over fifteen million people annually. Such figures have attracted the attention of water districts throughout the West, especially in California, resulting in economically motivated increases in funding for tamarisk control.

Tied up at this small beach is a park service raft marked *Weed Warrior*, and we stop to visit with two seasonal rangers participating in a grant-supported research project exploring ways to control tamarisk. They finish unloading steel tools in preparation for tomorrow's work, and I ask them what's next on the agenda.

"Oh, we'll probably have a few beers," says the woman, "but first we'll have to get our uniforms off."

"Isn't nudity against regulations?" I joke.

"Oh, I don't know," says the other ranger. "Some places I think it is required," he adds, flashing a smile.

"My husband is a law enforcement ranger," cautions the woman. "We didn't think anyone else was coming down river today," she says, changing the subject. "Otherwise we wouldn't have stopped here. We don't want people getting the wrong idea about camping in nondesignated sites. When we're done, we'll take a branch and feather out our footprints, so it looks as if no one has been here."

We wish them well and drift downriver. Steve is skeptical. "Isn't tamarisk part of the recent history of this place?" he mutters. The plan does seem a little odd: cut down the tamarisk, tear out the roots, pile everything above the high-water mark to cure, but pretend no one has been on the beach?

Tamarisk chokes beaches, and I hate it as much as the next boater. But this endeavor seems slightly mad. The stuff has a fierce will to live. Practically indestructible, tamarisk is a botanical rat. It can stay submerged for months and resprouts quickly after a fire. It can grow a hundred-foot taproot and tolerate soil salinity twenty times greater than the cottonwood seedlings it competes with. Adult trees produce a stunning five hundred thousand to one million seeds annually; seeds germinate in twenty-four hours. There are thousands of trees. An infantry division wouldn't get them all.

Perhaps that's why the park service and other agencies throughout the West are hoping beetles (*Diorhabda elongata*) imported from central China will help solve the problem. In theory, the bright yellow and black beetles and their larvae will eat tamarisk leaves, defoliating the trees and slowing their spread enough to make other eradication methods effective. The concern is whether the insects, released into Echo Park in 2006, can be controlled. The idea is that as tamarisk—the beetles' only food source—declines, so will their numbers.

Given the history of other introduced species, random gene mutation, and unpredictable evolutionary pressures, releasing hungry beetles seems the biological equivalent of storing fireworks next to gasoline.

Tamarisk eradication attempts reflect a desire to preserve the monument's ecological integrity by ensuring that native species and landscapes persevere. Eradication of tamarisk and other nonnative species, it seems to me, also reflects American desires for static "virginal" landscapes. Managing wilderness does not come without cost. In Dinosaur, for example, herbicides such as fluazifop-p-butyl, triclopyr, or sulfometuron-methyl are used to try to eliminate certain plants so that others can return. Some of these compounds have high soil mobility or high aquatic toxicity, meaning they travel through soil well, break down slowly, and have the potential to harm wildlife. Despite precautions taken by the park service, such herbicides can be absorbed into the food chain and contaminate water supplies.

Much of Dinosaur is pristine. But as I am coming to realize, managed wilderness is not truly wild. Americans seem to prefer managed replicas that act in predictable ways to the messy, often ugly Darwinian reality. On the other hand, nonnative species spread across 1.2 million acres of federal land each year, threatening endangered species and resulting in annual economic costs estimated at $137 billion in the United States. I'm not sure how to solve the problem. We could sit back and let nature take its course. But what becomes of desert places when flooded by this tide of invasive species?

The raft plods across flatwater. Filled with pinyon and two species of juniper—Rocky Mountain and Utah—Lodore is a canyon of trees in the high desert. Ponderosa pine and Douglas fir trespass below their normal elevation ranges of six to nine thousand feet, defying the conventional tree wisdom in the high desert and giving Lodore a surprisingly mountainous ambience. The ponderosa, for example, found along river level here and on the Yampa, are perhaps ancestors of stands present in the early Holocene, eleven thousand to eight thousand years ago, when the climate was cooler than today.

Soon we arrive at our designated campsite, a sandy bluff just upstream from Triplet Falls, where the river pinches down through a boulder-choked chute. Two weeks ago a ranger rowing the rapid for the first time flipped here. After unloading our raft, Steve sets off on foot to take some photographs, and in the velvety evening light he's soon engrossed in the nuances of filters, f-stops, and shutter speeds.

I hope to paddle through Triplet Falls, and unstrap from the raft the kayak we've been carrying. I drag the boat onto a beach and admire the entrance to Triplet Falls, where the river leaves the calm pool above. As the current accelerates, it forms a marvelous glassy green tongue of water leading into the rapid. Though I've logged several thousand miles as a commercial guide and private boater, the aesthetics and physical properties of rapids still fascinate me. I wedge myself into the kayak as the familiar satisfying scent of neoprene and dried river rises up. I snap on the spray skirt, push off, and do an eskimo roll to be sure I still can.

In the ocean, waves move through the water. Board surfers, after riding toward shore, must paddle back out to catch the next incoming wave. But on rivers, the wave form remains stationary as the water rushes through it, meaning paddlers can surf waves in place: Point the kayak's bow upstream, paddle, and find the exact spot on the wave where the motion of the boat gliding down the wave's upstream face is equalized by the current's downstream tug. Then surfing takes little effort. I find a small wave to surf, and soon everything fades until the only sensation left is the boat skimming the surface of the river.

Eventually I slip off the wave, find a calm spot beneath a cliff face,

Kayaker working upstream in Triplet, Green River, Canyon of Lodore

and crane my neck back to take in the steep narrow canyon. Visible near the canyon rim are bands of gray Madison Limestone. Formed during the Mississippian period, an era dominated by tropical seas, the rock marks the beginning of the transition to the limestone-dominated section of Lodore. In summer 1869, two determined members of Powell's crew scrambled twenty-seven hundred feet up the east wall to reach the canyon rim. An evening's re-creation of the historic ascent has merit in an abstract way. But the chirp of crickets and the low roar of whitewater fill the twilight canyon. There's no better place to be than right here.

I paddle to the bottom of Triplet Falls and try to surf another small wave. Afterward, I pull into a calm pool and mull over the wickedness of summer river trips. A one-week river trip is enough to get a little rest. Two weeks and I'm ready to go back to work. Three weeks and I start wondering why I work. Rivers are subversive for those trying to walk the straight and narrow.

HELL'S HALF MILE

In the early morning cool a park service patrol raft glides up. Doug, the ranger, is a dark wiry man with a whiskey rock-and-roll voice and an affinity for acrid unfiltered cigarettes kept in a small metal case. He's a sun-darkened old river cowboy who has rowed rafts across the West for decades with little gear. Minimalism. It's an underrated philosophy. Thoreau famously warned, "I think that the man is at a dead set who has got through a knot-hole or gateway where his sledge load of furniture cannot follow him." Ludwig Wittgenstein, now regarded as the greatest philosopher of the twentieth century, the son of a millionaire Austrian industrialist, gave away his vast inheritance. These guys would have known how to pack for a river trip. Consumerism, on the other hand, has changed rafting. "The

Wal-Mart phenomenon," Ranger Doug calls it: lanterns bright enough to illuminate convenience store parking lots, herds of aluminum folding chairs, tiki torches, and other made-in-China backyard clutter—stuff that insulates people from the very thing they seek.

Doug's my kind of old-school boater, a student of the region's hailstorms, flash floods, and big water. And he has a sharp eye for ecology, explaining how even regulation firepans—250 square inches—scorch the soil. "See this," he says, digging his finger into one of many darkened spots in the Triplet campsite. The dry soil is no longer ruddy brown, but blackened. He digs deeper. "See, it goes down deep, burning the organic material in the soil."

"Regulations only require a firepan," I say.

"Yeah. Firepans don't really protect the ecosystem, but they preserve aesthetics," says Doug. "That's what Americans like," he adds.

Steve and I spend the morning and part of the afternoon hanging out with Doug, and now we should get downriver. We thank Doug for his time and push the raft in, run Triplet cleanly, and start to worry about Hell's Half Mile. Hell's is Lodore's trickiest rapid, and like Warm Springs, another of the ten so-called big drops in the West. It's a place rich with river-running lore, and it waits less than a mile below.

Steve and I tie the boat at the top of the rapid and walk the pomegranate red scouting path worn by thousands of feet, including the members of two Powell expeditions. During the 1871 trip, the rugged Vicksburg veteran John F. Steward named the rapid while scouting. Today, with a rubber raft, the half-mile of whitewater seems less daunting than portaging tons of gear over the spill of boulders and then lining heavy boats down the drop—exactly what Powell's crew did.

Steve and I see a wave-filled channel bending right and dropping over a frothy ledge. Below it a VW bug–sized boulder nicknamed Lucifer blocks the current. It is a raft magnet, no simple thing to miss. The clean run is around the right side; plan B is to hit the rock head-on and spin off to the side. It's even possible we'll hit it sideways and have to highside—jump to the side of the raft next to the rock—to avoid a flip. That's plan C.

In late September 1909, the mustachioed Vernal trapper Nathan Galloway made the first recorded descent of Hell's Half Mile on an expedition with the Ohio millionaire Julius Stone. "Than," as his friends called the square-jawed Galloway, had perfected his stern-first rowing style by the late 1800s and was running rivers in his light flat-bottomed boats. Before him, in Powell's day, boatmen faced upstream, looked over their shoulders, and generally careened down rapids. Galloway's innovation changed that. By facing downstream and backing water against the current, standard practice today, obstacles could be seen and avoided.

With our scouting complete, Steve pushes us off. I take a couple oar strokes and drift down until it's time to row into position above the aerated tongue washing out of the bottom of the ledge. We drop over cleanly, but the current rudely shoves us toward the hippo-sized boulder. Time for plan B: straighten out, back water frantically, let the forward tube ride up on the rock, stay straight until we stop sliding up, then spin off. Nothing pretty, but we're through. "Oh, well," I say, heart pounding. In Hell's Half Mile, as in life, boaters don't always have a nice clean run. But part of the allure of whitewater and running a river multiple times is that occasionally, when water levels are ideal and the runs graceful, we can achieve a moment of perfection. Just not today.

a short time to be there: Echo Park

Below Hell's Half Mile, silvery late afternoon light spills through the canyon. Steve and I quietly float the final six miles of Lodore, as the red quartzite that dominated the canyon tapers to limestone, shale, and sandstone. The massive bulk of Steamboat Rock, named by the Powell expedition, swings into view, marking the entrance to Echo Park. As we drift past Steamboat Rock's seven-hundred-foot-high Weber Sandstone walls, the country opens up dramatically. The spaciousness, the creamy expanse of rock, the utter silence broken only by the murmur of water are the first things visitors to Echo Park notice. "It's a completely different river here," I marvel.

"A completely different planet," corrects Steve.

A short distance downstream, the Yampa joins the Green. We drag the raft onto a beach strewn with blood-red rocks. During the Yampa's spring flood, when the river carries upward of 10,000 cfs, this beach would be midstream. In May 1984 the river peaked close to a monstrous 35,000 cfs, the highest level since record-keeping began in 1904. Today, at this confluence of the free-flowing Yampa and the Green, tamed by Flaming Gorge Dam, the Yampa dribbles in a meager 200 cfs, a placid warm little stream at the bottom of a monumental canyon.

Not a bad spot. That's what hermit Pat Lynch thought after the Civil War, anyway. The eccentric scavenger who called Echo Park home for nearly fifty years became such a fixture that locals came to call Echo Park Pat's Hole, a name still found on maps. In this era of social services he'd be what we call homeless, shuffling dumpster to dumpster; but Pat, with his shrub of a beard, lived in high desert style, dining on jerked horse and mule deer carcasses and sleeping in caves. Sounds tempting. No price at all to live in a place like this.

We are lounging on the raft absorbing the high desert evening when a young ranger carrying his boots appears.

"Hey!" we say.

"Hey. Do you have a permit? I need to see it," he says. His name tag gleams in the evening sun. I can make out some sort of hyphenated name.

"Huh," I say, digging out the paperwork. "You're the second person who's checked our permit today."

He looks it over. "Going to Stateline?"

"Yeah."

"You have a permit for that?" he demands.

"What?" says Steve, confused.

"That." He points at the camera gear, especially the big telephoto lens.

Confluence of the Green and Yampa rivers, Echo Park

"You need a permit to shoot commercial photography in the monument," he says angrily. "It's a five-hundred-dollar fine if you're caught."

"We're working on a book for a university press," says Steve, "so it's not really commercial."

"A book is not commercial?" he says.

There's a long pause. "Well, it's for a university press," says Steve, finally.

"Everybody's telling the same story," the ranger says. "Just working on a small project." He stalks off down the beach.

"Traveling behind the Iron Curtain was less hassle," I grumble to Steve. Photography regulations are clear. We're not in violation of any of them. "I guess it's good to have some conflict," I venture.

"Doesn't bother me," says Steve, already over it. "That's the kind of thing you bottle up inside will give you a heart attack."

The behavior of this ranger is not reflective of most park service personnel, who handle well what is surely frustrating: the park service's dual mandate to preserve places while facilitating visitation. Despite our otherwise positive encounters with rangers, the fact that we've had our permit checked so often chafes at me. These traffic stops limit the potential river trips have to give people a break from their regimented lives off the river.

Downstream a group wades the slow current. The voices have the fast clip of a foreign language, French perhaps. I walk down the beach, unable to resist getting Europeans' impression of Pat's Hole. There are two families: women in sleek black bikinis, a bearded man in red shorts, the other man in skintight white underwear, three kids, a dog.

"Hi," I say, trying not to be intrusive, but astonished they're here. "Where are you from?" I ask, realizing too late that the bearded guy has the look of an American ski town dude.

"Steamboat," he says.

"We are from France," say the others.

"What do you think of this place?" I ask.

"Uh, magnificent!" says the man in the tight white briefs, sounding like Inspector Clouseau from *The Pink Panther*. "In the south of France now it would be one person next to another," he says, making a sideways chopping motion with his hand. "Belgians, English, Germans, too many."

"We complain if we see one or two people a day down here," I say, as much to myself as to them, realizing I may be overzealous in my quest for solitude.

I walk back to the Yampa's mouth and go upstream to where fine silt has settled and dried, forming a radiating pattern of cracks. I heft a chunk of the mud. Weighty as fudge, silky as chocolate mousse, the mud looks good enough to bite into. I stick my hand into its buttery smoothness. The easy evening light of the silent canyon, with its blond and rust-colored rock, beckons. I take off my swim trunks, ease myself into the warm mud, smearing my body with globs of dense sulfur-smelling glop. The slippery clay leaves grayish black swirls and my skin feeling supple and clean. It is royal treatment at a hermit's price.

Stone clatters loudly on rock and splashes into the water. Startled, I look up, expecting to see someone . . . but it is just rock falling.

Rock.

Cloud.

Sun.

Space.

Echo Park.

We are reluctant to leave, but camp is five miles downstream and sunset just an hour away—we'll be floating in the dark. The prow of Steamboat

Jenny Lind Rock, Echo Park

Rock appears as a runaway ship intent on beaching itself in sagebrush, slips past, and curious otters surface and dive near snarls of downed trees. The Green's current tears chunks from the riverbank, and every year the grassy open space of Echo Park diminishes. This is a side effect of Flaming Gorge Dam. Before the dam's construction the two rivers had fairly similar hydrological cycles, meaning they rose in spring and fell in summer. But now, the dam keeps the Green's flow artificially high during summer, fall, and winter. Since the Yampa is not dam controlled, its flow dwindles during those seasons. Now as the Green enters Echo Park from the north, there usually is not enough water flowing west out of the Yampa to deflect the Green's current away from the riverbank on the south. As a result, the Green now slices into the riverbank, badly eroding it.

The sun sinks below the canyon rim. We navigate disorderly, braided, sandbar-strewn channels that give Mitten Park a wild feel. Shadowy spires and fins of uplifted rock sweep around a warped outcropping at the mouth of Whirlpool Canyon. Farther in, we crane our necks upward to view sea stacks a half-billion years old that are evidence of ancient surf thundering against a rocky coast. Sea stacks are islands found near coastal areas, formed when headlands erode. As the ocean advances, softer formations erode, leaving harder vertical columns of rock standing offshore. Visible along the Oregon coast, for example, sea stacks are found throughout the world and time. Whirlpool Canyon's sea stacks are a visible reminder of the marine origins of Dinosaur's canyons.

We float past sheer polished Precambrian walls that drop straight to the water. I pull an oar out of the lock and sink the shaft underwater but cannot touch bottom. Deep. In spring, when the water is much higher, the river spins into the whirlpools that led the Powell expedition to give the canyon its name. Bats, perhaps silver haired, pallid, or Yuma myotis, flit and dart in the gloom, hunting insects, their wings ghostly translucent against the sky.

In the gathering night, we pass huge tumbles of boulders nozzled out of tiny side canyons with unimaginable force every so often, "often" being a relative term. All rapids in Dinosaur's canyons are caused by these alluvial fans, semicircular intrusions into the river channel, reminiscent of the trains of bridal gowns spilling across a floor. Eventually, Steve and I float in total darkness, following the light mutter of easy water, on guard for the deep bass note of heavy rapid. But the raft slips along under the stars without incident. We unload at Stateline campsite and sleep alfresco on the beach. After midnight, the wind drives sand into everything, leaving my mouth gritty and dry. It's a bracing shot of wildness.

Morning shadows fill the canyon as we break camp and float downstream toward Jones Hole Creek, where many commercial and private rafting parties are camped. As the sun rises, soft light begins to touch graceful arêtes, and bright spokes of light fall across the river. When Steve and I explored in January, this lower section of Whirlpool Canyon was sealed bank to bank in thick polished ice. Today, the current carries us out the canyon mouth and into Island Park with its stately cottonwoods, where the river meanders through hot, dry, open country that is the essence of the sagebrush West. Steve pushes hard at the oars across the flatwater and sandbar-strewn shallows.

Rafters congest the river below the Rainbow Park boat ramp, in part because day trips launch from here, putting more people on the water. A loud sunburned crew takes a group cigarette break just above Moonshine Rapid, the site of our raft flip years ago into cricket-infested river. I sense that the wilderness experience on this trip—if it ever existed for Steve and me—is over. The irony of protecting a river is that all too often it gets loved to death. There's a trade-off involved in preserving wild places, and the loss of solitude can be one of them.

Rafters in camp, Whirlpool Canyon, Green River

The commercial guides, too, sense the relaxed pace of their multiday trips are over, and row hard for the takeout. One, a blonde with long braided hair, shouts, "You guys gonna run any rapids in that kayak? Every time I see you, it's tied on the boat."

"Only the big stuff," retorts Steve.

"You do it, got to do it all," she says.

Why not? Steve takes the oars; I unstrap the kayak and seal launch off the raft into the river, where five miles of bony summer rapids wait. For adrenaline seekers they are a weak version of their full-strength spring selves, yet infinitely preferable to the reservoir that once threatened to drown this canyon. One hundred and fifty years ago, Powell knew water was the West's most valuable resource. Anyone afoot today in the red dirt sagebrush country, with its searing tandoori-oven midafternoon heat, would know exactly what Powell meant.

Nobody knew the value of water better than the Bureau of Reclamation. In the 1940s, it began planning the Colorado River Storage Project, a massive ten-dam effort that would turn spectacular desert canyons into reservoirs. Upper Basin projects included two dams in the monument. One, 525 feet high, would have gone in three miles downstream from the confluence at Echo Park, flooding it, the Canyon of Lodore, Browns Park, and Yampa Canyon. A second dam in Split Mountain Canyon would have submerged the rapids we now float, as well as Rainbow and Island Park. The very features that make Dinosaur special would have been obliterated.

Local interest in an Echo Park dam existed as early as 1946. Boosters hoped to bring water and power to the economically depressed Uinta Basin. Recreation opportunities and a tourist trade centered on easily accessible reservoirs were additional selling points. As river historian Roy Webb notes, the Bureau of Reclamation defined the monument with dams and reservoirs "in a way that those living nearby could understand, and this was something the National Park Service had never been able to do." A reservoir—a flat sheet of blue water—is easy to understand. Powerboats. Radios. Sunblock. No shift of perspective required. Muddy, turbulent rivers in inaccessible canyons are harder to comprehend. The value of their wildness, especially in 1946, was not quickly grasped.

Conservationists, however, adamantly opposed the dams. Led by the Sierra Club's David Brower, they set out to communicate the value of Dinosaur's canyons to the nation. If these projects were built, they asked, could wilderness areas continue to exist? Could any national park be kept free from development? The canyons' beauty and symbolic value as protected land ensured this would be no ordinary showdown over water. It was a litmus test that became a defining wilderness battle in American history.

Locals, western politicians, and the powerful Bureau of Reclamation supported the dam project. Easterners, water-hungry southern Californians, and wilderness advocates did not. For six years the canyons' fate was uncertain. Finally, when opponents threatened to contest every dam in the Colorado River Storage Project, the dams slated for Dinosaur were deleted from the legislation. Its rivers survived. But there was a trade-off: Flaming Gorge and parts of Red Canyon had to go under, as did all of Glen Canyon some two hundred-plus miles downstream. Today, as the possible draining of Lake Powell gets debated, it is clear that Colorado Basin desert canyons are inseparably connected to the larger bioregional tapestry. If Glen Canyon Dam is decommissioned, campaigns for new storage and diversion schemes will rise from the rubble. Flaming Gorge, for instance, has been mentioned as a water source for Utah's Wasatch Front, 120 miles distant.

As the Split Mountain takeout draws near, the canyon magic fades and the depression that accompanies the end of river trips sets in. By early afternoon the harsh Uinta Basin sun has fried up every last bit of shade. Outfitter trucks fill the concrete boat ramp at the mouth of Split Mountain Canyon, and paying guests cluster around shuttle vans. Our hot car waits in the parking lot. Long melted are the blocks of clear green ice the size of billiard tables that lay jumbled here in January, their water now evaporating out of Lake Powell.

Like many who float these canyons, we can't wait to do it again.

on the last free-flowing river: the Yampa River in August

River permits, time, and money being scarce, Steve and I wait a full year before we make another river trip. This time, we've come to explore the Yampa River by canoe during the August monsoon. Dinosaur, like the Sonoran Desert, receives precipitation from the monsoon, seasonally heavy rains that sweep the Southwest in summer. Tonight, at Deerlodge Park, mosquitoes, rising wind, and gauzy clouds presage moisture carried nearly a thousand miles from the Pacific Ocean.

Predictably, we wake to a steady rain. Not that I mind, as storms are one of the few truly wild things left, and inclement weather usually fills me with a strange joy. This storm further confirms that the six-year drought has broken, a fact that only increases my satisfaction. In the flat gray light, the deserted Deerlodge Park floodplain seems positively primitive. Like other put-ins, it evokes a disorienting feeling of transience. It is a place to cast off ties to the power grid, to mechanization, and to embrace rain, river, and rock. And for the next four days we'll be immersed in one of the West's finest canyons, that of the free-flowing Yampa.

Parallel lines etched into the riverbank mark the bearish trend of low summer water, and colossal sandbars plug the wide riverbed. Until Steve and I get the feel for the meandering channel, we drag the canoe as much as paddle it toward the canyon portal. Dark blue clouds lie heavy on the horizon, and a harder rain sets in. The steady murmur of water trickling across shoals and the hissing of raindrops immerse us in a world of boulder-choked rapids and near-constant rock gardens.

My sixteen-foot Old Town sat out the drought years, and I had forgotten how satisfying canoeing is. The boat glides like well-waxed skis across the calm stretches, cleaves the rapids' waves, and forgives unseen rocks. By noon Steve and I are well on the way to covering the twenty-two miles to tonight's camp at Big Joe Rapid. We are glad to do without the phlegmatic raft, with its rubbery processed-meat feel and clumsy oars.

The rain masks our scent, and we surprise three magnificent bull elk, symbols of the West, browsing along shore. The robust animals bolt uphill, where they become effectively camouflaged. Their hides blend with the rust-colored soil, and their heavy racks mimic the twist of dead juniper branches. The elk favor this stretch of river, as the easily eroded reddish Morgan Formation sandstone forms a broad gently contoured canyon, providing elk easy passage from the wild roadless country to the north, some of the most inaccessible in the monument.

The rain breaks up below Tepee Rapid. On shore, Steve and I dry our gear and, while exploring, find sandstone boulders dimpled with quartsize waterpockets, or *tinajas*, and antlers shed by elk.

Gear dried and repacked, we get back on the river and soon pass a syncline where layers of sedimentary rock droop over one another like a pastrami sandwich. We startle four more big-racked elk sure to find mates in the coming rut. Big Joe campsite appears around dinnertime, where Starvation Valley meets the river. These Yampa place-names seem the work of a country and western lyricist obsessed with misery: Dry Woman Canyon. Starvation Valley. Burnt Gulch. Disappointment Draw. Blind Canyon. Hell's Canyon. Vale of Tears. Why so much misfortune? Here, Weber Sandstone marries reddish layers of the Morgan Formation, and there is a peaceful camp above the mutter of rapid. But then at dusk, an evil black smudge builds to the south, trouble clouds. A gust of wind blazes through the underbrush, and soon the sandstone walls are awash in lightning. The rim brightens, silhouetted by blinding explosions as thunder groans through the canyon. As I crawl into the tent, I decide there might be a grain of truth in those names after all.

A heavy green tongue leads into Big Joe Rapid, now grotesquely swollen from the rain. Paralyzed with fear, but seeing no other option, we take our chances in the canoe on the powerful Grand Canyon–sized rapid. But then I awake, the sun is shining, the Big Joe of dream fades, replaced by only a trickle beneath piles of driftwood left by the spring flood, when the water ran fifty times higher than today, topping out at 14,100 cfs in late May. Today, under puffy clouds skipping across the arch of blue sky, our pace is more contemplative. Alternating silent floats in deep shade with gentle standing waves, the canyon soon opens into Harding Hole, the surrounding rock now exclusively the sublime Weber Sandstone.

After locating a spot to camp, we follow a trail up Bull Canyon to the canyon rim, seven hundred feet above the river. Below, petrified dunes of wind-etched rock, peppered with trees, fill the horizon. Billowing cumulonimbus drift as small storms scud off to the north, dropping rain. A gusty wind whips bristly pinyon. The wind has that fleeting, melancholy quality of a major seventh chord, with its need to find resolution. I close my eyes and lie in the pine's meager shade, soaking up this music as it seeks the tonic, feeling that summer is drawing to a close.

Later we descend the trail to the river and grab a quick dinner of sardines, crackers, and beer. Steve sets up for night photography, and I canoe across the river. A short hike takes me to Signature Cave, named for its inscriptions. As dusk falls, the commanding view from the cave offers a feeling of security. On my raft trip here eight years ago the overlook seemed scenic; it now seems strategic, perhaps like a marriage viewed in retrospect. The overhung cliff makes approach from above impossible; exposed narrow ledges on either side would expose intruders. Rocky Mountain bighorn (*Ovis canadensis*) love the spot, maybe for similar reasons. Four of them watch me carefully, their white noses piercing the gloom. I keep my distance from the heavy-racked rams.

Bushwhacking earlier today, I found pools of clear water in a steep side canyon; coyote scat and bighorn droppings lay in sheltered alcoves. Great Basin tribes used to drive bighorn into such sheer-walled box canyons, where hunters waited behind stone blinds. Below one likely spot, I found a translucent amber piece of flaked chert. With serrated knife-edged sides, it may have served as a scraper. Last night's storms must have uncovered this relic from a time when bighorn thrived from northern Mexico to British Columbia.

In the late nineteenth century excessive commercial hunting and disease spread by domestic sheep decimated Western bighorn populations. In Dinosaur, a combination of fire suppression, which allowed sagebrush and pinyon-juniper forests to overwhelm bighorn habitat, and parasites brought by domestic sheep proved especially devastating. Bighorn began dying off in the 1930s and essentially vanished from the monument by the late 1940s. Reintroduction began in 1952, when thirty-two bighorn were released in the Canyon of Lodore. Numbers increased, then declined in the mid-1970s, perhaps due to inbreeding. In 1984 and 2000, more bighorn were transplanted in Echo Park and near Tanks Peak southeast of Harding Hole. Currently, managers hope the animals will reestablish the historic altitudinal migration pattern that found them wintering along the river and summering in higher elevations.

An obstacle to bighorns' continued success are the oil and gas lease sales on state and federal land near the monument, including one parcel under the Green River itself. Bighorns are easily stressed by humans, and many oil and gas parcels overlap potential bighorn range. Energy development, with its roads, drilling pads, light pollution, and general industrial ugliness, fragments habitat and destroys the lands surrounding the monument essential to preserving its ecological integrity for future generations. But the government remains willing to sacrifice our scarce supply of remaining wild lands for a few hours of fuel. For the last ten years, the total annual average oil and gas production from all federal lands in Colorado met only 23.2 hours of the nation's annual energy needs. Utah's production meets little more than half that, at thirteen hours. The energy will soon be gone, but the impact of drilling will remain for generations.

Bats come weaving and darting out of the cave to feast on swarming mosquitoes, and I ease down to the cool air and pungent junipers along the river. Steve stays up all night photographing the spooky moonlight spilling into Harding Hole. Reason says one thing. The imagination feels ghosts of the long-vanished prehistoric Fremont returning to hear the murmur of water, the hypnotic rhythm of crickets.

We get on the river early next morning, and sun reflecting off water dances on undercuts, creating an illusion that the shimmering rock itself is liquid. Here, below Harding Hole, the river's character changes dramatically as it cuts through easily eroded Weber Sandstone. Gone are the steady rapids. The gradient drops from seventeen to seven feet per mile, and the Yampa swings through gooseneck meanders, a feature more commonly seen on rivers farther south, such as the Colorado and San Juan. We drift past inviting beaches, broad swaths of flood-deposited sand marked only by skeletons, the remains of fish snatched by predators out of the shallow shifting channel.

On this trip we see how most pre-dam Colorado Basin rivers once looked in August—shallow and warm. Remarkable fish evolved in the unique environment of warm low summer flows, varying levels of salinity, and cold turbid spring floods. But when the gates closed in December 1962 on Flaming Gorge Dam, four species endemic to the Colorado Basin began to decline. One of these was North America's largest minnow, the endangered Colorado pikeminnow (*Ptychocheilus lucius*), reaching six feet long and one hundred pounds. Its current main spawning area lies below a nearby sandstone dome called Cleopatra's Couch. Called "white salmon" by settlers because of its far-flung migrations, this predator continues to struggle for survival, in part because of the drought. The three-foot ten-pound razorback sucker (*Xyrauchen texanus*) and the humpback chub (*Gila cypha*), a specialized canyon species reliant on the Yampa for habitat, are also endangered. The bonytail chub (*Gila elegans*), a once-thriving species with an astounding half-century lifespan, is the most vulnerable. Nearly extinct, its survival depends on a hatchery program. For over three million years these fish lived here. We brought them to the edge of extinction in a half-century.

Harding Hole at night, Yampa River

After the flood: new growth along the Yampa River

What happened? Dams blocked migrations throughout the Colorado River system, reduced seasonal flooding essential to spawning, and lowered water temperatures year-round, making it easier for introduced species to compete in this altered environment. Before dams, some Colorado Basin rivers could warm to nearly one hundred degrees during the hottest midsummer months when the rivers were at their shallowest; today deep lakes form where the rivers back up behind the dams. Since turbine intakes lie beneath the surface where temperatures are colder, water released downstream usually starts out around fifty degrees, giving an advantage to the twenty-two introduced species found in Dinosaur. Species such as catfish, northern pike, and smallmouth bass continue to beat out endemic fish for food and territory.

Public opinion also factored. The bony flesh that once caused a Powell crewmember to complain that eating one of these warm-water fish was like chewing on a "paper of pins" often led twentieth-century fishermen to fling them into the undergrowth to rot, leading to the label "bush trout." Unfairly scorned as trash fish, these prehistoric survivors never enjoyed the political support that preserves habitat for cold water species such as trout. "Most people don't see their value and uniqueness," U.S. Fish and Wildlife Service biologist Mark Fuller told me this spring. "Each year we get closer to understanding their needs. But it's a race against time."

To aid recovery of warm-water fish, competitors such as bass and pike are electroshocked and removed from the monument as part of the Upper Colorado River Endangered Fish Recovery Program. Such measures border on the surreal, but the program gives endemic fish a chance if the Yampa remains free flowing—which is no sure thing. Development outside the monument, dam proposals, and energy projects that include coal and oil shale remind us that the Yampa's future is not secure.

Pushing these human worries aside, we anticipate the Grand Overhang,

Castle Park, and the final eleven miles, containing some of the Yampa's most dramatic canyon scenery. Summer's low water makes it possible to linger at the Grand Overhang, where an eleven-hundred-foot-high face angles over the river like an avalanche-ready cornice. An untimely earthquake might drop a slab of Weber Sandstone onto the raft, crushing us. These overhangs tend to get the better of my imagination, as at the famous Tiger Wall a few miles downstream, named for the dark vertical stripes across the rock's belly, left by intermittent runoff and rock varnish.

Downstream in Castle Park lies the former Mantle Ranch, recently sold to a new owner, and sandy spacious Mantle Cave, a major archaeological site. Found in the cave were tools, implements, fabrics, moccasins, pottery, and a complete feather headdress estimated to be over one thousand years old. Also found was a midden—perhaps belonging to enthusiastic meat lovers—that contained the bones of wood rats, striped skunks, and prairie dogs, as well as deer and sheep.

The evocative Weber Sandstone dominates this section of canyon, complemented by the fiery Morgan Formation reds. Warm Springs, with its seventeen-hundred-foot cliffs, nears. But we've not worried a bit about the legendary rapid, having scouted and run the other named rapids from the canoe. Yet the horizon line around the corner and the water's roar suggest we'd better have a look. And it's a different rapid than in springtime. From shore, Steve and I watch water tumbling through boulder sieves and over ledges. The narrow main chute splatters over rasplike rocks, making the technical rapid at least a class III. Whatever the rating, I know there's a 50 percent chance of flipping, having upset enough open canoes in whitewater to expect the worst. I dig out the helmets. A swim could be concussive.

We climb in the canoe and line up for the rapid, hoping for the best. If the sixteen-foot boat wrapped around a rock, and rope and pulley couldn't free it, we'd have to salvage our gear and wade to Echo Park. Twenty years

Scouting Warm Springs Rapid, Yampa River

Entering Echo Park, Yampa River

ago Steve watched me wreck a canoe in a similar spot, necessitating a walk out of the Adirondack woods, and he's determined to avoid a repeat. He draws the bow into the narrow channel, stabbing at the water, as I follow, swinging the stern through, like a hook and ladder truck down a city street. We go plunging down the tongue, burying in the soft water between the rocks, the clean line. We guide our half-swamped canoe to shore, where adrenaline sharpens every detail and etches it into memory.

Next morning, rock gardens expose long-drowned offerings to the Warm Springs river gods that include oar shafts snapped in two and a be-slimed but intact yellow Carlisle oar. Downstream the water glides through the final stretch of smooth sandstone canyon. Bighorns graze along cobble bars, flood-formed bars of sand and cobblestone-sized rocks. Blue herons slip along the shore until we reach Echo Park, on a morning so perfect it should go on forever. As the rivers join, the Green's fine brown silt billows like smoke through the clear Yampa.

We take out at the Echo Park boat ramp. Our car has been shuttled around from Deerlodge Park, and soon we are on a dirt road following Sand Canyon and the now-abandoned Chew Ranch. Once out of Echo Park, we pop up onto a stunning expanse of fire-restored native bunchgrass that sweeps to juniper-capped Weber Sandstone, pale beneath gathering thunderheads. Wind whistles through a mesmerizing Great Plains landscape of platinum, russet, and green, a vision of how the country looked prior to settlement. On the road's south side remains sagebrush-infested range, the result of decades of fire suppression and grazing. Proscribed burns can help native vegetation recover and restore this range to its original condition. But once a road is paved the country is never the same. As in Island Park, let's hope asphalt never touches this place.

the season of fading light: early winter on the Green River

Late October, and a fifty-year storm has unloaded heavy snow above eight thousand feet across the Wasatch and Uinta mountains. In the next few days, another twenty-four inches is likely. Flash flood, heavy snow, or winter storm warnings stretch from the Arizona state line three hundred miles north into Wyoming. Dinosaur lies in the precipitation shadow of the big ranges, but I keep an uneasy eye on the weather, wondering if we'll be rafting in a blizzard.

The drive east from Salt Lake across the Uinta Basin, with the high country visible to the north, plays in the lovely lonely minor key of the West. Before us stretches iconic western scenery—a meandering creek in the foreground, willows, sagebrush, and cottonwoods rising to rusty mesas and buttes, all backstopped by the gleaming Uintas, draped in wind-loaded snow.

When we finally arrive in Browns Park on the Uintas' eastern tip, the higher elevations are dusted with snow. Steve and I, along with old friend Sean Abbott, conscripted as trip cook, pitch our tents on ground muddy from an inch of rain, more than one-tenth the annual total. A great horned owl, one of nine owl species in the monument, hoots aggressively. Thick clouds converge on the towering Gates of Lodore, swallowing a bone white moon, and cottonwood leaves rattle hollowly in the wind. Change is in the air. I hoped for golden autumn days, summer yielding to fall, so that we might experience the Green River during a time of gentle transition. But winter is about to kick the door in. October can be a hard season, one requiring a similar hardening of the spirit. This trip offers a chance to experience the canyons and parks from a perspective different from that found during previous warm-weather trips.

Next morning brings brief respite from the storms, dawning dry and clear, with the temperature just above freezing. From yesterday's rain, the river's color is now that of liquid sandstone mixed with blood. Though Flaming Gorge Dam upstream controls the Green's flow, the river retains a measure of wildness during these wet periods, when its tributaries deliver water and sediment.

In down vest and wool hat, I rig the raft with childhood pal Sean, a big guy, blue eyed and bearded. Steve is photographing mule deer and keeping lookout for a bear cub spotted swimming across the river, and we have this part of Browns Park to ourselves. On this brisk morning, I see why indigenous peoples wintered here. The surrounding high country shelters the broad, semiarid valley from winter storms, yet there is abundant sunlight. As winter comes to higher elevations, game such as elk and mule deer move closer to the river, making hunting productive.

By midmorning we are close to having the raft rigged and loaded. I strap my kayak to the raft, and we set off on the river. A bleak, melancholy mood pervades as the raft enters the Gates of Lodore, the snow-dusted portal to the Canyon of Lodore. I feel the slow peeling away of city life, with its fast pace and incessant worry, and the hesitant late-autumn surrender to weather and geography. Steel-gray clouds begin grinding upriver, swallowing the sun. The canyon seems tough as gristle, like the nearby mountains, like the rugged steppe stretching into Wyoming.

"I don't mind the cold, but I hope it doesn't rain. I thought we'd get warmer weather," says Sean, who flew out west for the trip, hoping for a sunny break from his damp New England home.

"I figure four days of overcast, two with rain. Anything less is a bonus," I say. No one says anything, unconvinced by my apparent optimism. Privately, this trip seems a bad idea. My young daughter has the stomach flu and her mother is tending her alone. We argued about the timing of the trip. I'm fatigued from work and worried about the approaching cold front, severe enough, a ranger told us at the put-in, to cause other scheduled trips to cancel their launches.

We row past Wade and Curtis campsite, where Steve and I camped under a withering August sun. Summer's clattering woodpeckers and buzzing flies are long gone, and today the campsite seems a depressing tangle of mud and wood.

"It looks as if we are going downstream, but actually the waves are blowing upstream," Steve says, straining at the oars. Foot-high whitecaps slap against the raft, and Steve looks like he's trying to row a load of gravel across a parking lot. The notion that wilderness experiences are seasonal crosses my mind. During summer the Green River lacks the edginess I seek in wild country. Low water, sunny skies, and the presence of other people are the culprits. But fall is unpredictable and deserted. Nice.

The Canyon of Lodore seems to be holding its breath on this trip, waiting for the storm to deliver something—snow, a flash flood, deep cold. The possibilities are endless but the reality, especially water, limited. When we stop for lunch I hike to a rise above bone-dry Buster Basin Creek. The dominant impression is of rock, of waves and waves of rock lapping the horizon, dwarfing the river. At this moment, the Green seems a fragile wisp fed by unreliable tributaries. These dry washes and creeks, such as Buster Basin, are intriguing apparitions, measures of the desert's elusiveness. Like love or friendship, they can lie long dormant, awakening suddenly. I walk Buster Basin Creek, a deep dry slash in the sage-studded earth. Sometime in the last few days, a flash flood ripped through here, gouging the channel even deeper. Shreds of hide hang off a half-buried mule deer skeleton, crushed under a snowmobile-sized rock loosened by rain.

I rejoin Steve and Sean at the raft, and we float downstream to Pot Creek, tonight's campsite. Known as Cascade Creek prior to settlement, the creek once flowed into the Green. But upstream irrigators soon diverted its clear tumbling water toward Browns Park via Crouse Creek. Though the bed has been dry for decades, the lay of the land still says creek. Water etches a groove in memory as deeply as in these rocks, and with the scent of wet leaves heavy in the air, I suddenly miss autumn in the Adirondacks, with their forested rivers.

We unload the raft and set up tents on an inviting alluvial fan. Sean, the cook, lights the fire and sets to preparing dinner: beef, sautéed onion, chopped avocado, tomato, cheese, tortillas, beer. On this damp night the sweet taste of fat in meat seems illegal. I feel a little guilty, since cattle grazing does negatively impact this region, but tell myself there is little chance this beef came from the Colorado Basin: less than 5 percent of America's beef comes from cattle grazed on western public lands. New Jersey, for instance, produces more beef than Nevada; Mississippi more than Wyoming. But grazing remains the West's leading cause of water pollution and soil erosion.

Grazing once took place in over 90 percent of the monument, because many ranchers either owned land outright or had grazing rights within the monument before its expansions in 1938 and 1960, rights that were written into monument legislation. Today, nine permittees graze roughly 30 percent of the monument, over sixty thousand acres, and other herds graze allotments just outside monument boundaries. So-called livestock trespass incidents result when delinquent bovines wander onto nonpermitted monument lands. Most visits are accidental, but others less so. In the past, monument officials struggled to manage grazing's effect on native plants, animals, and riparian zones while trying to maintain a working relationship with ranchers.

Antigovernment sentiment can run high in the West, but most local ranchers and owners of inholdings—private lands held within monument boundaries—are now on good terms with the park service. Long-term negotiations resulted in agreements to keep cattle out of the river corridors. Land transfers at Cub Creek, and the buyout of animal management units in Rainbow Park, let the park service retire many grazing permits. Rangelands will continue to recover in the future as cattle are moved off these sensitive areas.

But for now, the impacts of cattle grazing remain. The Pot Creek area and the monument are covered in cheatgrass, an invasive species from the Mediterranean that was carried in imported grain shipments. Cheatgrass (*Bromus tectorum*) germinates earlier than native grasses, stealing the precious soil moisture native grasses need to thrive. Erosion is another consequence of grazing. On the monument's south side, for instance, much of Cub Creek has deteriorated into a flash-flood-scarred gully, a direct result of cattle trampling soil-stabilizing riparian vegetation. Archaeological sites are pressured; along the Cub Creek petroglyph site, cowpies lie scattered thick as cigarette butts at a bus stop.

Conflicts between private landowners and the mandates of the federal government are not unique to Dinosaur, but no discussion of ranching here is complete without considering the wrangling that existed for decades between some monument staff and the Mantle family who, in 1919, homesteaded scenic Castle Park along the Yampa. When the monument expanded in 1938, the Mantles' property fell within monument boundaries, but they retained title to the land.

The Mantles, who once contemplated building a full-service campground, ATV racetrack, and subdivisions on their inholding, understandably drew the ire of park officials. The Mantles also happened to irrigate from Redrock Spring, a local seep that 1926 USGS surveys placed on ranch property. Surveyors working in the 1980s situated the Mantles' spring box on federal land, and park service employees assigned to stop unauthorized use of federal resources demolished the diversion structure and filled the three-inch irrigation pipe with bentonite, a clay that swells and hardens when wet and that is used to seal landfills and nuclear waste dumps.

The Mantles, however, thought the 1926 surveys accurate, and they filed a lawsuit in Denver federal district court. First in time, first in line, as the saying goes, is the cardinal rule of Colorado water law, and at stake was the question of who had prior water rights: the Mantles or the federal government? The case had all the trappings of the old West: a judge leading a group on saddle horses to personally appraise the situation at the Mantles' ranch; testimony from a ninety-year-old woman said to have a "memory like a mule." The court eventually ruled in favor of the Mantles, due largely to the woman's testimony. In 1912, when she was just nine years old, recalled the woman, she had irrigated the orchard, field, and garden for Tom Blevins,

Cheatgrass along Pot Creek, Green River

a neighbor laid up with a broken leg. The irrigation water, she testified, came from Redrock Spring, a point that established prior use.

Ranching harms desert places across the West through its destruction of soils, impacts on native plants and animals, and degradation of water quality. But the greatest threat seems to me to be America's ever-increasing population. An energy boom threatens to double the population of nearby Vernal in the next decade. Given a choice between ranching and growth's one-way street, I'll take ranching, if it preserves open space.

After dinner, a cold drizzle sets in, and Steve, Sean, and I retire to the tents. In the middle of the night I jerk awake, feeling the heavy hand of claustrophobia. I unzip the rainfly and scramble outside for relief. But with the moon long gone, it is so dark I feel as if locked in a trunk. Knowing we're at the bottom of a narrow stretch of canyon doesn't help. Under a wet sky I try to imagine the river flowing into Echo Park ten miles distant, where my mind can unfold into its open spaces. The ambience of the Canyon of Lodore in autumn is even more somber than in summer.

Back on the raft next morning, we pass the remains of a powerful flood that occurred before Flaming Gorge Dam was built in 1962. Weathered tree trunks top boulders rising nearly two stories out of the water. Dread, veneration, and wonder: the Romantics' definition of awe. It's a fitting prelude to Hell's Half Mile, the class IV rapid that is Lodore's most difficult.

The familiar mix of anticipation and worry returns when we stop for the mandatory scout and walk downstream to have a look. Late fall is a time to be conservative, and a smooth run in the low water would be nice. But Hell's Half Mile will be tricky in our heavily loaded boat. Oar placement is crucial; catching the oar blade between two rocks would cause trouble.

On our return up the scouting path to the raft we encounter two men and a woman, tying up immaculate well-appointed catarafts.

"How you doing?" I say to a dark-haired woman who appears to be half-frozen. She stares blankly, says nothing. I repeat the greeting to a young man whose face has turned plum purple in the cold.

"Hey," he says, half-heartedly, apparently numbed by the weather.

Steve, Sean, and I untie our raft and bob down the wave train, but sure enough I crab an oar and take the ledge too far left, through the hole, and straight into the midstream boulder sometimes called Lucifer, pinballing off it onto another rock. And another. Messy. I pull the raft to shore and let out a sigh.

On his expedition with the Ohio millionaire Julius Stone in September 1909, Nathan Galloway, the Vernal, Utah-based trapper, single-handedly ran all four boats through Hell's, as he had upstream at Disaster Falls and Triplet. To justify the fun, he proclaimed in his journal, "I Runn the 4 boats thru + the Balance of the Crew Considers themselves Hardly Equal to the occasion," leaving them to portage the gear.

In his honor, but mostly to get a second jolt of adrenaline, I had unstrapped my kayak from the raft at the top of Hell's Half Mile and left it there so I could run the rapid again. Leaving Sean and Steve in the raft, I walk back upstream, and climb in the kayak. Hoping for one clean run, I slip through the waves and eddy into slack water behind the big boulder. Two strokes more and I plunge the boat over the rumbling ledge and past the troublesome boulder, then paddle over to rejoin the raft. I'm pleased to have finally made a clean run of Hell's Half Mile.

Blue sky flickers above, but the temperature plummets. The honking of Canada geese following the river south, that haunting chorus of creatures on the move, fills a now blackening sky. Soaking rain with wind is no joke in late October, and we row hard for Limestone campsite. Canyon walls above us glaze over first, and then the heavy precip catches us, covering the already saturated ground with a miserable layer of slush. The consolation prize is a stacked cord of *Weed Warrior*–cut tamarisk. I get the steel-plate firepan in a sheltered spot and carry up a few armfuls. Old-time backwoods campcraft bests the sodden wood and gusting wind, and a healthy fire is blazing in seconds. A single match is all that's needed. Well, that, and a half-quart of white gas, which produces a satisfying explosion.

After a wet cold night, I'm thinking again about the effect of weather on my perception of these canyons. In summer, Lodore's deep shade offers relief from the vermouth-dry sagebrush country, but this wintry weather makes narrow Lodore seem confining, and I can't wait to escape. Under a leaden sky, Steve, Sean, and I load the raft and row the last few miles to Echo Park, hoping for sun.

At the confluence of the Green and Yampa, sun breaks the clouds and showers golden cottonwoods with warmth. I shut my eyes and gratefully drink it in.

"Echo Park is not forbidding," says Steve. "You still have canyon, but it's welcoming."

"I am glad the sun came out," I say.

"I knew it would in here," Steve says.

But cliffs streaked with desert varnish soak up the light, and soon thick gray clouds plunge Echo Park again into gloom. We float past a small herd of mule deer and they begin stotting. These stiff four-legged jumps provide the animals with such sudden, unpredictable changes of direction that they will gang up on and strike predators such as coyotes. More commonly, though, stotting is an escape behavior that lets mule deer climb quickly, placing the ideal obstacle in pursuers' path: gravity.

The deer often feed with bighorn, and we count a twenty-head herd of sheep led by a heavy ram mounting a ewe. Moving as one entity like a school of fish, the bighorn seem collected and confident in the open park. This slant of autumn light puts creatures on the move in search of mates, browse, sun. I feel restless, too, wondering if I like these canyons best in bloom and warmth, but turn away in the darkening season. Yet October's fickle weather with its rain and wind, shadows and sun, at once brilliant and gloomy, depressing and uplifting, seems a more accurate reflection of human nature than summer's sunshine.

Multiple trips in every season can provide a rich sense of place in the monument. Like driftwood, memories from previous trips pile up, so that each experience in the present moment becomes illuminated by a similar one in the past. Running a particular rapid, hiking a favorite side canyon, observing animals, plants, and weather eventually becomes ritual. One repeats these things on each river trip, recalling prior experiences as eagerly as those in the future are anticipated. Floating Dinosaur's canyons suspends time's linear march as past, present, and future merge. That suspension is one of the many rewards of repeatedly exploring these canyons.

Of Fish, Fremont, and Floods

Before leaving Echo Park, we stop the raft and walk up Pool Creek Canyon to view petroglyphs. Faded images of bighorn, deer, a two-humped creature resembling a camel, an urn, an impressively two-penised figure, a snake, and a child speak across time in a celebration of life— virility, children, animals. The steady gurgle of Pool Creek fills the protected south-facing alcove. Away from the river's refrigerating effects, sunny fall or spring days would have provided warm conditions for pecking at the rock.

Desert varnish and Rocky Mountain bighorn, Echo Park

With perennial streams, side canyons such as Pool Creek attracted Fremont peoples—some nomadic, some farmers, some a little of both—who between AD 650 and 1250 inhabited the western Colorado Plateau to the eastern Great Basin. About one thousand years ago the Fremont era reached its apex, perhaps due to in-migration or climate change that forced drastic cultural reconfigurations.

Steve, Sean, and I return to the raft, and soon the river carries us into Whirlpool Canyon. In the shadow of the sheer walls, I realize the sublime canyon scenery that appeals to so many river runners may not have been preferable to indigenous peoples. Given the sunshine and clear streams of the warm game-rich parks and side canyons, it is easy to imagine that the indigenous preferred them to the dramatic but cold inner river canyons. I hadn't considered this aspect of place during the summer trip, but autumn offers a new perspective.

Explorers such as Nathan Galloway also enjoyed side canyons—especially for the abundance of fish found there. In the days when European capitals such as Vienna were awash in fin de siècle high culture—Klimt, Mahler, Freud—Galloway was running his expedition with Julius Stone. A few miles below Echo Park at Jones Hole Creek the trip stopped to do a little fishing. With old acquaintance Dubendorff, for whom a rapid in the Grand Canyon was named, Galloway caught (and kept) ninety-eight fat native cutthroat trout.

As in Galloway's day, Jones Hole Creek still flows south into Whirlpool Canyon, bubbling up from limestone springs just outside the monument. Calcium carbonate dissolved from the limestone precipitates any suspended particles that would otherwise cloud the water, keeping it perfectly clear except during spring runoff, periods of rain, or flash floods, when flow and turbidity increase.

This sparkling creek entices trout confined to the concrete tanks plunked down amid the asphalt of the National Fish Hatchery adjacent to the monument. In a piscine adaptation of Jack London's *The Call of the Wild*, a few brave souls flop out of the tanks, across the pavement and into the stream. Some misfortunate ones leap the wrong way, ending up out on the tar, crisp as smoked sardines. But even the lucky gamblers who strike out for something besides the monotony of food pellets and right angles, generally find themselves on the wrong end of a No. 12 fly, their instincts dulled by hatchery life. Wild fish struggle too. Native cutthroats compete with these escaped newcomers—browns from Europe, brookies from eastern Canada, rainbows from the Pacific Northwest. Migration of species, whether native or introduced, is similar to the migration of humans—irrepressible, and often destructive.

Jones Hole provides spectacular hiking, and one February day I decided to make the drive over from Salt Lake City. Up on Diamond Mountain deep snows drifted across the Jones Hole access road, Great Plains style, but lower elevations were largely snow free, and the eight-mile round-trip hike from the fish hatchery seemed doable before dark.

My first stop was Deluge Shelter, an important archaeological site high above Jones Hole Creek. Long shadows had already spilled into the canyon when I arrived at the site, hard up against a cliff and deep in shade. Archaeologists believe indigenous peoples did not inhabit Deluge Shelter during winter, when sunnier sites offered more pleasant living conditions. But it otherwise received heavy use. During excavations in 1966, archaeologists found evidence that people used this site for over eight thousand years. Fifteen separate cultural layers down to a level of five meters contained firepits, pottery, tools such as metates, and weapons such as spears, atlatls, and arrow points.

Generally, artifacts tend to be segregated by geography in and around the monument. In the eastern parts of the monument and north of monument boundaries, big-game-hunting northwestern Plains cultures dominated. Regions west of the major archaeological sites in Castle Park on the Yampa River, however, show the presence of Great Basin desert cultures.

As an archaeological site, Deluge Shelter is unusual because it reveals a cultural overlap. Plains, desert, and intermontane cultures all took advantage of the site's shelter, proximity to water, and defensive location at the base of a cliff. Deluge Shelter is also significant because it may help explain the disappearance of the Fremont. Excavating archaeologist Larry Leach found a "thick layer of sterile wind-deposited sands" above the Fremont layers. The layer of sand contained evidence of only short-term habitation, implying that an extremely dry period may have hastened the demise of the Fremont and led them to abandon Deluge Shelter. Unfortunately the artifacts that might have yielded further clues are gone. During the 1966 excavation season, the archaeological team camped south of Deluge Shelter, where Ely Creek enters Jones Hole from the west. A violent canyonwide flash flood swept down Jones Hole Creek and washed away the artifacts stored at the camp. One of the few places untouched was the excavation site, henceforth called Deluge Shelter.

On this late February afternoon the empty pit seemed as melancholy as a failed farm. All that remains at the site are pictographs and petrogylphs, but I noticed that vandals had used the images for target practice, leaving some pockmarked. The shadows grew colder, and I walked the Jones Hole Creek trail south to the Ely Creek campsite, where the flash flood swept through nearly forty years ago. I followed a snow-covered trail up narrow Ely Creek and around a trickling waterfall to the looming form of Cathedral Spire. Smooth sandstone canyons resembling twisting European alleyways branched off in several directions. Snug, inviting, with springs and running water, these Ely Creek canyons also appealed to indigenous peoples, whose skeletons and artifacts were unearthed by archaeologists.

I retraced my steps back to Jones Hole Creek, and then turned south until the creek's murmur joined the Green's heavier voice. Despite the beauty of Jones Hole, I felt drawn to the big river, perhaps because it appealed to my own innate restlessness; with a boat I could simply get on the river and leave my life behind for a while. Or perhaps the attraction came from the comforting sense of returning to a familiar thing—the river itself, where the illusion of timelessness offered an antidote to the disquieting notion that time is forever slipping away.

Afternoon ebbed and I returned up the creek toward the fish hatchery. Daggers of desert varnish dissolved into the dusk, and cold white stars appeared. Darkness swallowed the icy rock-strewn trail, and I had to let my feet find the way. Jets rumbled across the sky, a lonely sound on a midwinter night. Like Echo Park, Jones Hole is a place of confluences. Of creeks and rivers, certainly. Of cultures, rocks, seasons, too.

These memories slip away, as does today's October afternoon, and soon Steve, Sean, and I are through Whirlpool Canyon. Petrified sand dunes, evidence of the vast Saharan-type desert covering the region some two hundred million years ago, darken as a soft purplish hue washes Island Park. Virga, rain that evaporates before it reaches the ground, trails across the sky, reminiscent of a Romantic-era landscape painting. In this season of fading light, Island Park's wild, volatile beauty emerges.

We tie up at the Big Island campsite and carry gear through the sagebrush to a dirt patch beneath a gnarled cottonwood. Gusting wind soon showers the wet night with sparks from the campfire, and ragged curtains of rain continue to move across the darkened hills of Island and Rainbow parks.

Fog near Big Island in October, Green River

Eventually a nearly full moon rises above Whirlpool Canyon, silhouetting leafless cottonwoods against jagged canyon walls. The faint light gives the landscape the eerie quality of a photographic negative, of something gone by. During my river guiding years, late October was the season when life thinned out, as camaraderie and whitewater faded. Away from rivers my senses dulled until the spell of moving water was just a dim memory by the gray edge of November.

Next morning we awake to find distant buttes dusted with snow. Shafts of light scatter across Island and Rainbow parks, places that once seemed a mean combination of flatwater, wind, and heat. No longer. These vast western spaces, once featureless to me, now seem knowable. Mist rises off the river, where the raft beckons for the last time this year. Rain-soaked bluffs steam, forming fog that hangs across the surrounding hills.

From rivers, everything in Dinosaur National Monument follows.

bibliography

Belknap, Buzz, and Loie Belknap Evans. *Dinosaur River Guide*. Evergreen, CO: Westwater Books, 1997.

Dellenbaugh, Frederick S. *A Canyon Voyage: The Narrative of the Second Powell Expedition Down the Green-Colorado River from Wyoming, and the Explorations on Land, in the Years 1871 and 1872*. 1908. Reprint, New Haven, CT: Yale University Press, 1962.

Dinosaur National Monument Invasive Plant Management Plan and Environmental Assessment. U.S. Department of the Interior, National Park Service. Dinosaur National Monument, October 2005.

Fradkin, Philip L. *Sagebrush Country: Land and the American West*. New York: Knopf, 1989.

Galloway, Nathan. Diary of the Galloway–Stone River Expedition, 1909. Western Waters Diary Collection. Marriott Library, University of Utah, Salt Lake City.

Geist, Valerius. *Mule Deer Country*. Minocqua, WI: NorthWord Press, 1989.

Hansen, Wallace R. *Dinosaur's Restless Rivers and Craggy Canyon Walls*. Vernal, UT: Dinosaur Nature Association, 1996.

Harvey, Mark W. T. *A Symbol of Wilderness: Echo Park and the American Conservation Movement*. Albuquerque: University of New Mexico Press, 1994.

Hemingway, Ernest. *A Farewell to Arms*. 1929. Reprint, New York: Charles Scribner's Sons, 1957.

Jacobs, Lynn. *Waste of the West: Public Lands Ranching*. Tucson, AZ: Lynn Jacobs, 1991.

Kolb, Ellsworth L. *Through the Grand Canyon from Wyoming to Mexico*. 1914. Reprint, New York: Macmillan, 1952.

Leach, Larry. *Archaeological Investigations of Deluge Shelter, Dinosaur National Monument*. Boulder: University of Colorado, March 1967.

Madsen, David. B. *Exploring the Fremont*. Salt Lake City: University of Utah Press, 1989.

Monson, Gale, and Lowell Sumner, eds. *The Desert Bighorn: Its Life History, Ecology, and Management*. Tucson: University of Arizona Press, 1980.

Nash, Roderick. *The Big Drops*. Boulder, CO: Johnson Books, 1989.

Powell, John Wesley. *Canyons of the Colorado*. 1895. Reprint, New York: Argosy-Antiquarian, 1964.

———. *The Exploration of the Colorado River and Its Canyons*. Introduction by Wallace Stegner. 1895. Reprint, New York: Penguin, 1987.

Staveley, Gaylord. *Broken Waters Sing: Rediscovering Two Great Rivers of the West*. Boston: Little, Brown and Company, 1971.

Stegner, Wallace, ed. *This Is Dinosaur: Echo Park Country and Its Magic Rivers*. New York: Knopf, 1955.

Stone, Julius F. *Canyon Country: The Romance of a Drop of Water and a Grain of Sand*. London: G. P. Putnam's Sons, 1932.

Tennent, William L. *John Jarvie of Browns Park*. Cultural Resource Series, no. 7. Vernal, UT: U.S. Department of the Interior, Bureau of Land Management, 1981.

Untermann, G. E., and B. R. Untermann. *Popular Guide to the Geology of Dinosaur National Monument*. Dinosaur National Monument: Dinosaur Nature Association, 1969.

Valdez, Raul, and Paul R. Krausman, eds. *Mountain Sheep of North America*. Tucson: University of Arizona Press, 1999.

Velez de Escalante, Silvestre. *The Dominguez-Escalante Journal: Their Expedition through Colorado, Utah, Arizona, and New Mexico in 1776*. Salt Lake City: University of Utah Press, 1985.

Webb, Roy. *The Call of the Colorado*. Moscow, ID: University of Idaho Press, 1994.

———. *If We Had a Boat: Green River Explorers, Adventurers, and Runners*. Salt Lake City: University of Utah Press, 1986.

Wuerthner, George, and Mollie Matteson, eds. *Welfare Ranching: The Subsidized Destruction of the American West*. Washington DC: Island Press, 2002.

Zwinger, Ann. *Run, River, Run: A Naturalist's Journey Down One of the Great Rivers of the American West*. Tucson: University of Arizona Press, 1984.

about the author

Hal Crimmel is a former river guide and has paddled or rowed over one hundred different rivers in the United States and abroad. His essays on outdoor-related topics have appeared in *Pacific Northwest Quarterly*, *South Dakota Review*, *ISLE*, and *Paddler*. He is a former Fulbright Scholar to Austria and the editor of *Teaching in the Field: Working with Students in the Outdoor Classroom*.

about the photographer

Steve Gaffney is a portrait and fine art photographer based in Manhattan Beach, California. He has published photographs in national and regional publications, and his work can be seen at www.stevegaffney.com. Although he's at ease on alpine rock routes and in big ocean surf, it took him a couple days to get his bearings in the rapids of Lodore. This is his first book.

Library of Congress Cataloging-in-Publication Data

Crimmel, Hal, 1966–
  Dinosaur : four seasons on the Green and Yampa
rivers / text by Hal Crimmel ; photographs by Steve
Gaffney.
       p. cm. — (Desert places)
  Includes bibliographical references.
  ISBN 978-0-8165-2430-3 (pbk. : alk. paper)
    1. Natural history—Dinosaur National Monument
(Colo. and Utah). 2. Dinosaur National Monument
(Colo. and Utah). I. Gaffney, Steve, 1966– II. Title.
QH76.5.D76C75 2007
508.788'12—dc22   2007029360